SPEECH OF HON. C. C. CLAY, JR.,

ON

SLAVERY ISSUES,

DELIVERED AT

HUNTSVILLE, ALABAMA, SEPTEMBER 5TH, 1859.

CORRESPONDENCE.

HUNTSVILLE, Monday, Sept. 5, 1859.

ON. C. C. CLAY, JR.:

EAR SIR:—The undersigned listened with great pleas- to your masterly speech, delivered in the Court se this morning; and endorsing, as we cordially do, sentiments expressed and believing that your fellow zens in other portions of the State, who did not en- the pleasure of hearing you, will derive both plea- and instruction from a perusal and study of your ch, we request a copy of it for publication.

We have the honor to remain
Yours respectfully,

. H. SCRUGGS,	WM. FLEMING,
PEETE,	L. P. WALKER,
. SCOTT,	ROBT. FEARN,
WALLACE,	I. A. LANIER,
. GILL SHORTER, of Eufaula.	E. D. TRACY,
	W. W. GARTH,
. COLCOCK,	W. J. SAFFOLD,
BEN CHAPMAN,	STEPHEN W. HARRIS.

HUNTSVILLE, Sept. 6, 1859.

ENTLEMEN:—I am highly honored, as well as gratifi- by your note of yesterday, endorsing the sentiments my speech, and requesting a copy of it for publication. t was unwritten, and my language, for the most part, remeditated, I cannot report it literally, but can, my notes, present the facts, and arguments used, will endeavor to do so, after the lapse of a week or days. Other engagements will prevent an earlier pliance with your request.

I have the honor to be
Your fellow citizen,
C. C. CLAY, JR.

essrs. J. H. SCRUGGS, S. PEETE, S. S. SCOTT, WM. MING, L. P. WALKER, and others.

SPEECH.

ALABAMIANS: I salute you as fellow-citizens, stituents and friends. Fellow-citizens of United States, which, whether contempla- in its material or moral aspect, deserves, as as received from foreign nations, the name GREAT REPUBLIC! Fellow-citizens of one of thirty-three free, sovereign and independent States, composing a confede- ration, not a consolidation, a union, not a na- tion called the United States. Constituents, whom it is my pride and honor to represent in that high council-chamber of sovereignties, the Sen- ate of the United States! Friends—for such, I trust, you all are, either personally or political- ly—many of you friends of my childhood and manhood, to whom I am indebted for all the honors I have enjoyed. Friends, constituents, fellow-citizens of Alabama and of the United States: These are the chords that bind me to you, and I name them in the order of their strength. I'am attached to you as citizens of the United States, for it is, according to our fathers' covenant, *our* country, for whose "com- mon defence and general welfare" all patriots should labor. I am more attached to you as fellow-citizens of Alabama, for to her I owe my first, last and highest allegiance. I am yet more attached to you as constituents, for I am your honored servant, as well as fellow-citizen, to whose hands the rights, interests and honor of Alabama are confided. But I am most at- tached to you as friends, for who can define the duties and obligations of friendship?

I come to speak of principles, not persons, of measures, not men; and if in my unpremeditat- ed language my words should grate harshly upon the ears of any, I trust it will not be re- garded as intentionally offensive.

I appear by request to speak of that ever- recurring, interminable and all-absorbing theme of SLAVERY, as your counselor, not your cham- pion. I should not have volunteered to counsel you, for nothing is more difficult to any but a vain man, or more dangerous to any but a des- perate politician, than to advise the people how to act in great emergencies. To magnify my embarrassment, I am forewarned, by some Democratic presses and leaders, that the principles and sentiments, entertained by me and avowed last winter, have been already condemned by a majority of that party and of the people of this State. Every man has more or less respect for public opinion and desire for public approbation; and it too often happens, that those holding or seeking office adopt public opinion and court public approbation regardless of their own principles or of popular rights. I respect public opinion, but my own conscience more. I desire public approbation, and while holding office, will strive to merit it; but never, never will I surrender my principles to popular clamor or the dictation of any party. Many of you know, that from my youth I have lived a Democrat of the straitest sect. I am, have always been, and expect ever to be, a *States' Rights* Democrat. I never was, am not and never will be a *National* Democrat. This declaration may put me out of the pale of the Democratic party, as threatened by some of its professed organs, but hear before you strike, you uncalculating and real Democrats, who follow party for the public weal and not for pelf or power. *That word National does not belong* properly to the political vocabulary of this country. The framers of the Constitution and of the Union rejected it. It has been foisted into our party nomenclature by those who would convert the general government of the United States into a consolidated democracy, and has been ignorantly or carelessly accepted or tolerated by many strict constructionists and true States' Rights men. It is unfortunate that the Convention that framed the Constitution sat in secret, that its proceedings were carefully concealed for many years, and are now but imperfectly revealed. Had it been open to all to hear and report its debates, the government would have started and the people would have kept it in the right direction.—None would then have been guilty of such phrases as the *National* Government, the *National* Congress, or the *National* Democratic party. To prove this I invoke the aid of history.

A meeting of deputies from several States, at Annapolis, in 1786, recommended the appointment of Commissioners "to devise such *further* provisions, as shall appear to them necessary to render *the constitution of the federal government* adequate to the exigencies of the *Union.*" The Congress of the Confederation, in 1787, recommended a convention of Delegates, to be appointed by the States, "as the most probable means of establishing in these States a *firm National* government"—thus expressing a wish to exchange the then *federal* for a *national* government. Fearing, probably, to wound the pride of the States, Congress added another object of the Convention to be, to "render the *federal* constitution adequate to the exigencies of government." Each of the twelve States that sent Deputies, replied to these discordant recommendations by rejecting the proposed *National* and by authorizing the intimated *federal* government. The credentials of the deputies define their duties. They are before me, but one will speak the purposes and principles of all. The credentials from Massachusetts were "for the sole purpose of revising the articles of Confederation, to render *the federal constitution* adequate to the preservation of the *Union.*"—Such is, substantially, the language of the credentials from each state. All exclude the word *National* and use the word *Federal*; thereby showing that the States knew the difference between a *National* and a *Federal* government and chose the latter. Yet, strange to tell, notwithstanding the express instructions to form a *federal* government, on the day the convention met, 29th May 1787, Mr. Randolph, of Va.—the State which had been the herald and pioneer of free republican government—moved resolutions, proposing that *national* government which his own and every other State had refused to authorize the Convention to frame! He proposed *a national executive, national judiciary and national legislature*, which legislature "shall have the right to legislate in all cases in which the harmony of the U. S. may be interrupted by the exercise *of individual legislation*, and *to negative all laws passed by the several states*, contravening in *the opinion of the national legislature*, the articles of the union or any treaty under the Union." This resolution will suffice to show what was to be the character of the *national* government. Mr. Randolph, when advocating them, said, "his resolutions were *not intended for a federal government; he meant a strong consolidated union, in which the idea of states should be nearly annihilated.*" Mr. Madison said that by the "resolve of having a *national* government" "it was then *intended to operate the exclusion of a federal government.*"—Judge Read, said "*A state government is incompatible with a national government.*" Mr. Hamilton, said, "*we must establish a general and national government and annihilate the state distinctions and state operations. I believe the British government forms the best model the world ever produced*" * * * "and this truth *gradually gains ground.*"

It did gain ground so far that it was resolved to adopt the *national* form, giving to a *national* legislature power to revise and annul state laws and to supervise and direct the domestic interests of the people; thus making the States dependent provinces of a central, consolidated, *national* government. Nothing but fear of its rejection by the States, and the heroic opposition of the deputies from Connecticut and New Jersey, prevented the convention from finally adopting such a government, and caused it to obey instructions and frame our *federal* constitution. Mr. Patterson, of N. J., said: "Let territories of Nebraska and Kansas. The act, just quoted, said so, in declaring that restriction "inoperative and void," because "inconsistent with the principle of non-intervention by Congress with slavery in the States and territories as recognized by the legislation of 1850." It cured the wrong by undoing what had been done against slavery, and, to prevent like wrong in future, explained its "true intent and meaning" to be. "not to legislate slavery into any territory or State, nor to exclude it therefrom."—When? How? In organizing territories, by applying to them Ordinances of '87 or Missouri restrictions or Wilmot Provisos, or in refusing admission to slaveholding States, as done in the case of Missouri, and attempted in the cases of Arkansas, Florida and Texas.

Certainly, the history of Congressional intervention and the definition of non-intervention given by that act, both prove that it only pledged Congress not to intervene as to slavery by legislating it out, (as it had done,) or by legislating it into any state or territory—which was falsely charged to be the meaning of repealing the Missouri Restriction.

But Mr. Douglas lately declared, it was intended to empower the territories to legislate slavery into or out of them, and to bind Congress not to hinder or restrain them, no matter what might be their legislation, whether constitutional or unconstitutional, just or unjust, righteous or wrongful! Most discreditable acknowledgment of his own purpose, and unjust attribution of an unworthy purpose to the State Rights men of the South who aided in passing that act!

Did he proclaim that to be "the intent and meaning," or his own intent and meaning, pending the discussions of the act in 1854-5-6?—He was its author, and in justice to himself, as well as to its Southern supporters, should have told them, if he so intended: gentlemen, this bill, if it become a law, will install "Squatter Sovereignty" in those territories, and authorize it, "by non-action or unfriendly legislation" to abolish or prohibit slavery therein, notwithstanding the federal Constitution may be thereby violated and your States rights' annulled; and you hereby pledge yourselves never to ask Congressional intervention against any invasion of your rights, by those "sovereigns," however fatal, flagrant or unconstitutional? Far from giving them, as he does now, this interpretation of that act, he induced the belief by his course, votes, speeches and reports, before introducing the Nebraska-Kansas bill, pending its consideration, and, subsequently, up to his canvass in Illinois in 1857, that he dissented from Gen. Cass's theory of territorial or "squatter sovereignty." He voted, on 26 Feb'y, 1849, in the Senate, for the Walker amendment giving the President almost unlimited power, *executive, legislative* and *judicial*, over the internal affairs of our newly acquired Mexican territories; thereby evincing exceeding contempt for sovereignty in territories and entire confidence in the power and duty of Congress to govern them. In the very bill he offered for organizing Nebraska—Kansas territories, the sovereignty of their inhabitants was plainly denied and their entire subordination to Congress clearly asserted. That act created their governments; named all their officers—Governor, Judges, Dist. Attorney, Marshal—made them mere creatures of the President, (appointable and removable by him) and of Congress (on whom made dependent for their pay;) provided for supporting the civil list out of the federal treasury; gave the President's appointee, their governor, a veto of their legislation; and, in short, treating them as mere dependants and beneficiaries, gave them a charter defining their powers and directing them to obey it. Thus, their inferiority and subjection to Congress was assumed by the bill itself, whose author now claims for them the powers of sovereignty—yea, powers greater than those of their creator, Congress, or than any State legislature!.

Pending the discussion of his bill, Mr. Douglas, altho' often declaiming in favor of popular sovereignty, never advocated territorial or squatter sovereignty, or declared these words implied the same thing; or, indeed, defined either. Gen. Cass did not dissemble his opinion, but frankly declared his belief of the sovereignty of the inhabitants (or people, as he styled them) of a territory over persons and property within its limits, as an inherent or natural right, and entirely consistent with the Constitution. Every Southern Senator, I think, repudiated the idea of such sovereignty, and many denied that Congress could, or did, by that bill, confer any sovereign power over property, or delegate any power it might not reclaim. On 15 Feby. 1854, Sen. Brown of Miss., said:

"*I have not, in my own judgment, and I trust I have not in my action here, yielded the principle that the people of the territories, during their territorial existence, have the right to exclude slavery. I have not intended to yield that point, and I do not mean that my action in future times shall be so construed.*"

Sen. Douglas moved to postpone the bill [Nebraska Kansas] till to-morow.

Gen. Cass asked him to withdraw the motion and said: "The Hon. Sen. [*Mr. Brown*] has touched on one of the main questions connected with it, and which has not been touched before. It is a very grave and a very important question. The power of the people of the Territories to legislate upon their internal concerns, during the period of these temporary governments, is most clearly given in this bill, if the Constitution permits it."

"Mr. Badger. Certainly."

Mr. Cass. If the Constitution does not permit, they have not got it.

Mr. Badger. That is clear.

Mr. Cass. Behind that stands the other question which must be discussed here; and I, for one, am determined that my constituents shall know my views on the point. It is one on which the Hon. Senator from Miss., and myself differ. * * It is whether, by virtue of the Constitution of the U. S., there is a kind of motive power in slavery that immediately spreads it over any territory, or by virtue of which any slave may be taken to any territory of the United States as soon as it is annexed * * * * *

Mr. Butler. I wish to save myself. I am perfectly willing to vote for the clause [that quoted by me] as modified by the Hon. Sen. from Ill., the chairman of the committee on Territories [Mr. Douglas,] but with a very clear judgment that, if Congress has not constitutional competency to legislate either one way or the other—either to introduce or prohibit slavery in the territories a territorial government has no derivative authority to do so from any act which Congress can pass.

Mr Brown. Certainly not.

Mr. Butler. I am perfectly willing to leave this question under the constitution.

Mr. Dawson. That is where it ought to be left.

Mr. Butler. I am perfectly willing to leave it under the Constitution, to be decided by the law tribunals of the country; and that is where it ought to be left. If in process of settlement, the people of these territories shall be prepared to assume upon themselves the attributes of a sovereign state, they can then, certainly, either exclude or admit slavery.. I presume that will not be denied by any one. During their growth and before they undertake to become a state, can they assume to exercise a power which Congress itself, under the Constitution, cannot confer upon them? They can have no derivative power on the subject from an act of ours."

Mr. Cass. That is a matter to be argued. I differ from the Hon. Senator *in toto.*

Mr. Douglas did not say he differed from him *in toto* or in part. On 24th Feb. 1854, Mr. Brown spoke at length in support of his and Mr. Butler's position; quoting the authority of Mr. Calhoun, that "the territory is open to all citizens of the U. S., and *must remain open and cannot be closed but by the people of the territory* WHEN THEY COME TO FORM THEIR OWN CONSTITUTION; declaring that in voting "to leave *the people perfectly free to form and regulate their domestic institutions in their own way, subject only to the Constitution of the U. S.,*" he gave no more right to destroy the domestic relation of master and slave than that of parent and child or husband and wife.

"I deny [said he] that the right to *regulate* carries "along with it the right to *destroy*. The right to regu-"late the relation between master and servant no more "entitles the regulating power to destroy that relation "than does the power to regulate the relation between "husband and wife authorize destruction of that relation. "As well might the territorial legislature take a wife "from her husband, under pretence of regulating their "relations, as to take a servant from his master under "pretence of regulating that relation. * * *If I* "*thought that, in voting for the bill as it now stands,* "*I was conceding the right of the people in the territo-*"*ry, during their territorial existence, to exclude sla-*"*very, I would withhold my vote.*"

He added, that he was willing to leave the question of territorial power, as provided by the bill, to the decision of the Supreme Court. Senators Butler, Hunter, Mason, and others might be quoted to the same effect; but the views of Senators Brown and Butler show those of all Southern States Rights' men who voted for the bill.

Was it not the duty of Senator Douglas, the author of the bill and its leading advocate, when those able and candid men gave their interpretation of its meaning, to correct them if they erred? He knew the great interests of the South, in their opinion, could only be maintained by the bill as interpreted by them, and would be as effectually destroyed by squatter-sovereign powers as by the Wilmot Proviso; and he knew their deep solicitude to secure the South against both, and the hope of doing so, by passing his bill. If a true friend to them, or the South, would he not have saved them from the fatal pit which he saw them approaching, by saying: 'You misunderstand the meaning of the bill; I wrote it and ought to know its purpose and effect, and I assure you Gen. Cass's construction of it is correct?' Was it the part of a faithful ally to dig the pit, conceal it and lead them into it? The same power was given in the same sentence and same words over *all* the domestic relations—"*to form and regulate*" *them* "*in their own way, subject only to the Constitution of the United States.*" Surely, by no fair construction could power be derived under those words, "form and regulate," to destroy, or abolish, or prohibit the domestic relations of husband, father, or master; and, yet, more surely, no greater power was given thereby over that of master and servant than over the other domestic relations.—That was the opinion and argument of Southern Senators who supported the bill. But, we now are given reasons for thinking those words a delusion and a snare! Ah! we are adjured, yea commanded, even by Southern men, by our love of the Union and the "National Democracy," to hush murmurings, hide the fraud, abide the treachery, and take the consequences!

But you may ask, how could you and other Southern Senators vote for that delegation of power over the domestic institutions to the territories, when Gen. Cass, said their Legislatures might, in virtue thereof, get power to prohibit or abolish slavery? Because he qualified that assertion by those potential words, "*if the Constitution permits it,*" and immediately added, "*if the Constitution does not permit, they have not got it.* Mr. Badger said "that is clear," and all thought that none would deny it, who reverenced the Constitution. Although I thought and think Gen. Cass's opinion of territorial sovereignty a mischievous heresy, I thought and think him a patriot and honest man, who would not only submit to, but support, the Constitution of his country. We gave no powers that were not "*subject only to the Constitution of the United States.*" Those words served as an amalgam to unite Northern and Southern pro-slavery, and anti-slavery, pro-squatter and anti-squatter-sovereignty men, who reverenced the Constitution, and meant to sustain it. All professed to be willing to leave it, "under the Constitution, *to be decided by the law-tribunals of the country,"* whether Congress, or its creature, a territorial legislature, could prohibit or abolish slavery in the common territory of the States of the Union. And, as Senator Benjamin said, last winter, in the Senate, in reply to Senator Douglas:

"Nobody anticipated at the time, that after this final settlement, an attempt would be made to legislate in opposition to the principle settled by the Supreme Court; and, of course, *no member from the South could for a moment, have entertained the idea of the Senator from Illinois, that the people of the Territory, after the decision of the question in favor of the South, should have the right to legislate in opposition to the principle thus guaranteed.*"

Nobody then even dreamed that Mr. Douglas would ever tolerate such iniquitous and atrocious usurpation of power by a territorial legislature. On the contrary, he heard the declations of Senators, in 1854, just quoted, as well as similar avowals from other Senators, that the legislature of Kansas could have and exercise no power, beyond that given by Congress, or inconsistent with the Constitution, and never expressed a dissenting opinion. He heard Senator Butler, on 25th February, 1854, say further:

"I know, sir, that it has been said, that we are parting with a great power in giving the people of the territories the right to regulate their own concerns, according to their own opinions, independent of the control of Congress. I admit of no such principle. Justice to myself, the honest conviction of my own mind, as well as the authority of great minds, who have expressed themselves on this subject, will never allow me to assent to the doctrine that the first comers upon the soil of a territory can appropriate it, and become sovereigns over it. No, sir, the Federal Government stands in the relation of a guardian to a ward. Look at the bill as it stands. It prescribes government for the people of Nebraska and Kansas; but, if this spontaneous, this inherent popular sovereignty is to spring up the moment the people settle in a territory, and assemble to form a government, why have any bill to put them into operation at all?—You give them a chart and say they must obey it. Suppose that the first act you get from the territory of Nebraska or Kansas, is one declaring that no slaveholder shall be eligible to office in either of those territories, or that no one professing the Catholic religion, or that no Jew shall be eligible to office, or that the Mormons shall have a preference, would you tolerate it? According to some notions that I have heard expressed, having put this machinery of government in operation, you have no power to control it. In other words, it is contended, that though a territorial government is one under a power of attorney, emanating from a principal, yet, as soon as the power of attorney is signed by the principal, it becomes irrevocable, and that then the attorney can do anything which he pleases, without the controlling or revoking power of the principal. If that were the case, I might hesitate to trust the people with the unlimited powers which some seem to think have been devolved on them in this bill, but WHICH CANNOT BE IMPLIED, EITHER FROM THE OPINIONS EXPRESSED HERE, OR FROM THE DESIGNS OF THE BILL ITSELF."

Why did Sen. Douglas suffer that frank and noble man, who disdained to deceive others, thus unwittingly, to deceive himself? Why permit that gallant patriot, who lived and would have died for his mother State, unconsciously to commend the poisoned chalice to her lips, with persuasive words of filial piety? Gentlemen, Mr. Douglas did not intend to mingle the poison in our cup that he has lately found there. He was not the *particeps criminis* to that horrible parricide he would now impute to us. I do not believe he meant to betray us to the ruin of our States and the South, and inveigle us into the violation of our oaths to support the Constitution, by delegating unconstitutional powers, or pledging ourselves to suffer our agent, the territorial legislature, to exert unconstitutional powers even against our own States. The South was the party wronged and injured, for whose redress the Nebraska-Kansas bill was introduced. Her Senators, representing her interests, accepted the remedy tendered by Mr. Douglas, telling him what they believed it was and how it would operate and he silently acquiesced in their interpretation. Sen. Butler, speaking for the South, said to him, 'by your bill we give the Legislatures of Kansas and Nebraska a chart and say they must obey it—they are our agents, whom we may and must control?' Sen. Douglas did not gainsay this construction of his bill, and is bound by it, both by legal and by moral principles. He has changed, not Southern supporters of his bill.

Again, Sen. Douglas, himself, denied the sovereignty of a territory and asserted its subordination to the will of Congress, in a report made by him to the Senate, in March, 1856, in which he said:

"The sovereignty of a Territory remains in *abeyance suspended in the United States, in trust for the people until they shall be admitted into the Union as a state.—In the meantime,* they are admitted to enjoy and exercise all the rights and privileges of self-government, *in subordination to the Constitution* of the U. S. and *in obedience to the organic law*, passed by Congress in pursuance of that instrument. These rights and privileges, are all derived from the constitution, through the act of Congress, and must be exercised and enjoyed in subjection to all the limitations and restrictions which that Constitution imposes."

In April, 1856, Sen. Brown, commenting on this report said:

"And if, as is pertinently said in another part of the same report, "the rights and privileges" of the people of the Territory "are all derived from the Constitution *thro' the acts of Congress*" and "they have no inherent sovereign right to annul the laws" which Congress has given them, it becomes equally clear, that they have no authority, derived from any quarter, either the Constitution, the acts of congress, or the God of nature, during their period of territorial existence, to exclude slavery. Such is my understanding of the report; *such I believe to be the true intent and meaning of its author;* and, *so understanding* and *so believing*, I give to the report my cordial and unqualified endorsement and approval."

Mr. Douglas accepted this compliment as his just due, and tacitly acknowledged that "to be the true intent and meaning of its author," himself.

On 12 June, 1857, when canvassing Illinois, he repelled the idea of territorial sovereignty and asserted the doctrine of Sen. Butler, that the territorial government is our agent, whom

Congress may and must control, by declaring in favor of repealing the organic act of Utah, "blotting the territorial government out of existence," "bringing it under the sole and exclusive jurisdiction of the U. S.," "in order that persons and property may be protected, and justice administered, and crimes punished under the laws prescribed by Congress in such cases."

He attempted to avoid the inconsistency of his views of the power and duty of Congress towards Utah and towards Kansas, when presented to the Senate, on 23 February last, by Sen. Green, in these words: "In the case of Utah, he wanted persons and property protected." * * "To do that, he wanted Congress to intervene and *protect property*. Now, in the most palpable case in which slave property may be destroyed in Kansas and Nebraska, he says we have no right to interfere." Mr. Douglas, replied, "I argued that we ought to repeal the organic act [of Utah] because they were aliens enemies and outlaws; not on account of their religion; not on account of their domestic institutions; I never expressed any opinion as to what we ought to do in regard to their domestic institutions; but I would repeal that act because they were in a state of rebellion, defying the authority of the U. S."

Well, under the authority of the United States, declared in the Constitution, as expounded by the U. S. Supreme Court, you may carry and hold slaves in Kansas. What could be more rebellious or defiant of that authority, than for the Territorial legislature to destroy your property?—refusing citizens of the U. S. the enjoyment of a right guarantied by the highest law of the land—the Constitution?—Circumstances alter cases: in this case our ox is gored, in that of Utah the Northern ox is gored.

I trust I have shown by the political history of intervention, and of non-intervention, as expressed in the Compromise measures of '50 and the Nebraska-Kansas act of '54, as construed by Southern supporters, and even by Mr. Douglas, its author, that the South did not thereby concede Squatter Sovereignty, or territorial Sovereignty, or the right of Territorial legislatures to use the sovereign power of abolishing, prohibiting or destroying rights of property, free from any restraint by the Constitutional guardian, the Congress of the U. S. Such a concession by Southern Senators can only be made to appear by garbling their speeches and presenting some glittering generalities or careless expressions about "popular sovereignty" or "leaving the question to be settled by the Supreme Court." I hold in my hand a pamphlet copy of so much of the late debate in U. S. Senate between Mr. Douglas and others, as suits his purpose, to which are appended extracts, which he says he believes "to be fair and impartial," tending to fortify his assertion of that concession. He prudently omits his mocking challenge to us, to try to intervene to protect our property from confiscation by Brown and Lane's party in Kansas. Every Southern Senator in '54, who took part in the debate of Feb. last, denied that he made or intended to make that concession, in the Nebraska—Kansas bill; yet Sen. D., by those extracts tries to prove the falseness or error of their assertions. And some presses, with those unfair and partial extracts, furnished them by him, are engaged in the unenviable work of sustaining him and his late construction, by defaming them and trying to show how they intentionally bartered Southern Rights and abdicated their sworn duty to defend them by authorizing Territorial Legislatures to violate them at pleasure. He and they have put in that dishonorable category (by use of one of those partial extracts) A. P. Butler, who never 'paltered in a double sense,' or changed his course for popular favor or presidential preferment. If you knew the men, you would stake the word of the dead Butler against that of the living Douglas. Yet those presses not only discredit him, but Benjamin, Davis, Brown, Hunter, Mason, Green—yea, all the Southern States rights Senators, in order to prop up Mr. Douglas while pulling down the very keystone of our federal fabric, the equality of the States and of the people!

But, say the supporters of Judge Douglas, there is a Badger-Proviso, pledging Congress not to intervene, either to protect, establish, prohibit or abolish slavery. It does not; but it does say that "nothing herein contained shall be construed to revive or put in force any law or regulation which may have existed, prior to the act of 6th March, 1820, either protecting, establishing, prohibiting or abolishing slavery." What law or regulation? The French or Spanish law, existing in 1803, when we acquired the Territory? Northern men said: 'we repeal the Missouri restriction, thereby conceding your right to enter Kansas, with slave property; but that will be construed to revive the old French and Spanish Slave Codes and thereby legislate Slavery into it; and you ought not to ask us to do that.' Southern men replied, 'oh, no, we have just said, by the Douglas amendment, we do not intend or mean by this act to legislate slavery into any territory, and, therefore, even according to the rule of common law, it would not revive those laws; but by the civil law, under which slavery existed in those Territories in 1803, the repeal of a repealing statute does not revive the former law; and, therefore, it would be mere tautology to repeat that we do not intend to legislate Slavery into Kansas.'—Our Northern allies replied, then, save us against the false charge of Abolitionists by adopting this Proviso. And, for that purpose, Mr. Badger offered the Proviso, prepared by the life, liberty and happiness of man. To protect it, men unite under a common government, that may establish a Law, to be acknowledged by all as the rule of their controversies, to be expounded by Judges, to be defered to by all, and enforced by an executive, to be submitted to by all. It is for the protection of property that allegiance is due, and when protection ceases allegiance ceases. No freeman will support a government that does not protect him.

It is unconstitutional doctrine. Congress cannot define property except money—or discharge any article from being property. All powers delegated to it, or prohibited, were delegated or prohibited to protect persons or property—and to secure equal protection to citizens of each and every State. Hence, all of our governments, state and federal, are inhibited from *taking private property for public use, without just compensation—from making unreasonable searches or seizures of the property of the people —from taking life, liberty or property, without due process of law.* Hence, to prevent Congress from abusing rights of property of any state or class of citizens, to benefit another state or class or citizens, it is provided, that all duties, imposts and excises shall be *uniform* throughout the United States—that no capitation or other direct tax shall be laid unless in proportion to the census—that no *preference* shall be given by any regulation of commerce, or revenue to the ports of one state over those of another—all bankrupt laws shall be *uniform* throughout the U. S.—citizens of each State shall be entitled to all privileges and immunities of citizens in the several states—the enumerations in the Constitution of certain rights shall not be construed to deny or disparage others retained by the people—the powers not delegated by the Constitution to the U. S., nor prohibited by it to the people are reserved to the States, respectively, or to the people.

While every guard that wisdom could conceive or express was thrown around private property, equal care was taken to secure equality to the States in the use and enjoyment of public property. Every power given Congress is declared to be "for the common defence and general welfare"—that is the defense and welfare of each and every State, equally and alike. And respecting the territory and other property of the U. S., it is declared, that "nothing in this Constitution shall be so construed as to prejudice any claims of the United States, or of any particular State." Of all property none was so carefully guarded asthat of slaves. It alone, of all property, was given representation, both in Congress and in the President: thereby pledging both President and Congress to guard and protect; for why give it a voice in legislation, if it was to be dumb, or a hand if it was to be paralyzed, when its rights were assailed! Congress is pledged to protect it by calling forth the militia to suppress insurrection—by preventing each State from destroying or impairing it, by any law or regulation discharging from service any slave that may escape into it, or from not delivering him up on claim of his master—by restraining Congress from prohibing the importation of negro slaves for twenty years, or till 1808, or imposing a tax or duty exceeding $10 for each slave. Here, let me digress a moment to say, that I deprecate the discussion of the question of repealing the foreign slave trade laws, and will not take part in it, because it tends to distract the counsels and divide the strength of the South, at a time when rights of immediate and vital importance are assailed: but I will say publicly, what I have privately, that it is unfortunate for the peace of the country, that the States did not reserve exclusive control of the foreign, as well as inter state, slave trade, and while power was given by that clause, to prohibit importation of slaves after 1807, I think Congress exceeded its power in declaring and punishing as piracy the taking or receiving of negroes on a foreign shore, with intent to make them slaves. While the last clause was under discussion in the federal convention, George Mason, of Va., urged as a reason for immediate prohibition of the foreign slave trade, the probable spread of slavery over the territories west of Va., N. C. Ga., now forming the slaveholding States of Ky., Tenn., Miss., and Ala. Alluding to the prohibition of that trade by Va., and Maryland, he said: "All this will be in vain, if South Carolina and Georgia be at liberty to import. The Western people are already calling out for slaves for their new lands and will fill all that country with slaves, if they can be gotten through South Carolina and Georgia." But the framers of the Constitution refused to prevent its expansion over the territories. Thus while strong guards were thrown around private property, generally, especial and extraordinary protection was provided for property in slaves, by making it an element of federal power, recognizing it as property to be taxed, to be imported, to be delivered up on claim of the master, to be represented in Congress and in the President, and to be restrained from insurrection, by Congress through the militia. And to secure justice and equality to all the States, respecting public property it was provided, that, in disposing of the Territory or other property of the United States, it should be done with strict regard to the claims of each and every State and for the equal benefit of each and every State. Therefore, in the language of Mr. Calhoun—the greatest intellect, in my opinion, that this country has produced—"if the Territories belong to the United States, if the ownership, dominion and sovereignty over them be in the States of the Union, then neither the Territories, nor their legislature can exercise any power but what is subordinate to them. But if the reverse be true, if the dominion and sovereignty over the territories be in the inhabitants * * they might exclude whom they pleased and what they pleased. But in that case, they would cease to be territories of the United States, the moment we acquired them and permitted them to be inhabited. The first half dozen squatters would become the sovereigns, with full dominion and sovereignty over "them."

Here then is a right of entry into the common territory of the U. S., and a right of protection of property there by Congress, guaranteed by the Constitution, as declared by the Supreme Court,—to whose decision "all good citizens should submit"—that we must surrender, I am told for the sake of our northern allies and the preservation of the Democratic party of the Union. Judge Douglas demands its surrender, and his Southern supporters request it. They say it is an abstract right, of no practical value. If so, it has become so by the expulsion of slavery from Kansas by domestic violence, and legislative menaces. On the 23rd February last, Sen. Green, stated in the Senate, that the territorial legislature of Kansas had passed an act declaring, that from and after its date, slavery should cease to exist in Kansas. Sen. Douglas, with seeeming joy and triumph, thereupon mocked us with the question; "When will the time for Congressional interference come, if manumitting all your slaves and confiscating all your property does not constitute sufficient cause for prompt action?" The act did not become a law, and effect what he shouted over too soon, because the Federal Governor did not approve this "unfriendly legislation." It is no mere abstract right, in Kansas, according to the testimony of Senators and other prominent men, who from personal knowledge assure me slave labor there would be more profitable than in Alabama. But the value of the principle is far greater than that of territories or slaves,—it is inestimable. The corner stone of our political in stitutions is protection of persons and property. We are asked to yield this right of protection by Congress, in the common territories, to consent to outlawry there, to endure the manumission of our slaves and confiscation of our property,' without asking redress or remedy of Congress, and be patient under the mockery of professed friends and foes in the North when we complain of such wrongs!

If our Northern allies demand or request this, they ask or require too much of their equals—more than magnanimous men would claim of their inferiors. It is an insult to the South to make such a demand or request. It is an insult to her Representatives to charge them with abdicating the power, or abnegating the duty, of protection of her property by Congress. If they did so by the Kansas act, it is to that extent null and void, because unconstitutional, and the South is not bound by it, and should not abide it. If they did so ignorantly or wilfully, they are unworthy of your confidence and you should withdraw the trust so unfortunately confided to them. If you yield this demand, it will prove an irreparable injury.—You cannot do it without sinking into deserved inferiority and degradation. You will not do it, if the spirit of your sires still lives in their sons.

The Federal flag that floats over Northern property in every sea, is an ensign of its protection. For that protection we fought the war of 1812—scourged the Mediterranean pirates and the Barbary States for harboring them—drove the South Sea buccaneers from their hiding-places—bombarded and demolished Greytown—demanded and extorted from Austrian despotism the surrender of Martin Kostza, a foreigner, who had taken only initiatory steps towards his naturalization here. Yea, the free negroes of Liberia, sent there by the misguided philanthropy of colonizationists, beneath that flag find shelter and protection for their persons and property against the attacks of their barbarous brethren of Africa, at the expense of federal treasure, ¾ths of which is collected from the South! And while protection is afforded to Northern men and foreigners and even free negroes, on the high seas or foreign shores, shall it be denied to Southern men, in their own fields and by their own fire-sides, at home, in the common territories of the United States! Never, never, by my consent.

I feel the respect and attachment that is due to the Northern Democracy, who have proven their fidelity to us and loyalty to our commen Constitution in the past. I believe it to be the only Northern party from which we can hope for anything we desire, and when we separate from them, we sever the last link of federal, miscalled National, parties, and, perhaps, the strongest ligament of the Union itself. I know that that party, now reduced to a small minority in the North and beleagured by our and their foes, is menaced with destruction. While contemplating their past power and present weakness, the exultant declaration of the resolute leader of those foes, Mr. Seward, uttered in my hearing eighteen months ago, recurs to me.

> "All parties (said he) in this country that have tolerated the extension of slavery, except one, has perished for that error already. That last one—the Democratic party—is hurrying on, irretrievably, toward the same fate."

To preserve our allies, by acceding to the demand of Mr. Seward, the acknowledged leader of our enemies, Congress must prohibit. To preserve them, according to the demand of Mr.

Douglas, Congress must not protect. Coming from a professed ally and friend, this proposition is not less odious and offensive than that of our enemy. Mr. Seward denies your right to protection in the territories by any power, Federal, Territorial or State, and gives you fair warning, that if you enter them, you shall be robbed of your property. Mr. Douglas admits your right, throws open the territories by repeal of all prohibitions, and invites you to enter, but authorizes squatter-sovereignty to prepare a pitfall for your destruction, and promises to stand by, not merely a passive spectator, but an active abettor, to arrest the protecting hand of your constitutional guardian, the Congress of the United States. Give me an open enemy rather than a treacherous ally. To consent to either proposition is to submit to dishonor and ruin. Protection in the enjoyment of equal rights and privileges of persons and property, was the purpose of the Union and pledge of the Constitution. If any party refuse it, to any section or State of the Union, let it die. If the Federal Government, under the control of the North, refuse it to the South, or under the control of the South refuse it to the North, the bond that connects us is thereby broken, and the injured section can have no worthy motive for preserving the Union. The exaction of support without affording protection, is the extremest tyranny of government. I trust, the South is not willing to submit to it. I hope, the Democracy of the North are not willing to demand it. Certainly, Mr. Douglas, although their able and honored leader for several years past, cannot bring them to demand of us concessions, which would be fatal to us and fruitless to them.

I need not now tell you, that I will not support Mr. Douglas or any one on his platform, although nominated by the unanimous vote of the Charleston Convention, of the Democratic party, or any other party whatever.—I love the Democratic party for its principles. I will not abandon those principles for policy. I prefer the right, even with defeat, to the expedient, with success. I prefer truth to triumph. I love the Union of the constitution—a Union of equal, independent and sovereign States; but I love my native State, "my nursing mother and my grave," yet more; and I should be a faithless and dishonored guardian of her rights, did I consent to abdicate the power and abandon the duty of Congress to protect the property of her citizens, whenever or by whomsoever assailed, wherever the federal flag floats. Protection is an inherent right of citizenship, guarantied by the Federal Constitution, as expounded by the Federal Supreme Court, and when you surrender it, you will cease to be freemen and to deserve the rights, privileges and immunities of freemen. As your trustee and servant, I will not do so, at the bidding of squatter-sovereignty, National Democracy or State Rights Democracy—yea, at the bidding of the Legislature or the people of Alabama. If commanded to do so, I will resign my trust, retire to the deepest seclusion of private life, and hiding my face in shame and humiliation and sealing my lips with silence about such cheap and worthless things as State rights or fremen's rights, become a quiet passenger on the ill-fated bark of the South, as it drifts ingloriously down the stream of Time into the black and tideless sea of infamy and oblivion.

---

*Since this speech was delivered I have read Mr. D.'s article in Harper in which he clearly asserts the supremacy of the Territorial Legislature, within its limits, over both Federal and State governments.

DEMOCRAT PRINT,—HUNTSVILLE, ALABAMA.

us consider with what powers we are sent here. By our credentials we see, that the basis of our present authority is founded on a revision of the articles of the present confederation, and to alter and amend them in such parts where they appear defective. Can we on this ground form a *national* government? We are met here as deputies of thirteen *independent and sovereign states for federal purposes*. Can we *consolidate their sovereignty and form one nation;* and annihilate the sovereignties of our states who sent us here?"

Mr. Sherman and Judge Ellsworth, of Conn., vigorously supported Mr. Patterson, aided by a minority of the convention. Mr. Lansing declared: "Had the legislature of N. Y. apprehended that their powers would have been construed to extend to the formation of a *national* government, no delegates would have appeared on the part of that state. *New plans, annihilating the rights of the states,* (unless upon evident necessity) can never succeed." I might quote other extracts from the debates, showing that the federal Convention was divided into two parties, the *nationalists*, who favored a consolidated democracy of an American *nation*, with absolute power in the majority of Congress to control the affairs of states and people, and the *federalists*, who wished to preserve the independence and sovereignty of the States, and limit the powers of Congress to matters of *common* interest, mainly *external* to the States.—The *federal* party ultimately triumphed over the *national* and formed a confederation not a consolidation, an union not a nation; and, appropriately, called the charter of its powers, the Constitution of the *United States* of America. They carefully expurgated it of the term *national*, and of every synonymous word, and adopted throughout the precise language to convey the idea of a *federal* system.

Now, mark and take warning of these facts: The *large States favored the consolidated* or NATIONAL *government*, the *small States the limited* FEDERAL form; showing the universal inclination of the strong to increase their power, and the natural repugnance of the weak to entrusting the strong with power. I doubt not the patriotism of Randolph, Hamilton, Madison, and other advocates of a *National* government.—They thought it necessary to keep the States together and enable them to resist foreign aggression, and they trusted to the magnanimity of the great States not to abuse the interests of their weaker sisters. I doubt not that many patriots are now Nationalists.

This same division of States and of parties, into advocates of national and advocates of federal powers of government, has continued ever since, and exists to-day. The *Nationalists* of the Federal Convention dropped that name, immediately on the adoption of the Constitution, and took that of their opponents, and all were Federalists during the Administration of Washington. But, still, many nationalists at heart, though federalists by profession, by arrogating for Congress *National* powers and exercising them in adopting the Alien and Sedition laws, made the name federalist odious, although a good word, expressive of the true nature of our government. Hence, the real federalists formed a new anti-national party, called *Republican*, under the lead of Thomas Jefferson. He and Mr. Calhoun always called themselves Republicans. That was the original States' Rights Democratic party name, and it is to be regretted that it was not adhered to and is not now the name of the States Rights' Democracy, because our States are really Republics, not Democracies, and their general government is an Union of Republics, not a National Democracy.

The majority party in the North, miscalling itself Republican, termed by us Black Republican, would make our general government a National Democracy if they could. They claim for it national powers over domestic interests and private and public property. They claim absolute power over the territories and other property of the U. S., over the District of Columbia, dock-yards, forts, arsenals, navy yards, &c.; and, therefore, insist that Congress should prohibit or abolish slavery in all those places. They claim power in Congress to discriminate in favor of Northern against Southern interests, in many other ways; as by protective tariffs, fishing bounties, ship-building monopolies, coasting-trade monopolies, pensions, internal improvements, foreign mail steamer-monopolies, donations of public lands in free farms, insane asylums and agricultural colleges. By such measures the Northern States (or a majority party in them) would consolidate or nationalize the federal government, aggrandize themselves and impoverish and oppress the South. They can control Congress, for they have a majority of six votes in the Senate and of fifty-seven in the House of Representatives, with assurance of ever increasing majorities, and, like the large States in the federal convention, they do not fear their own power and would enlarge it illimitably. On the contrary, the majority party in the Southern States, like the small States of that Convention, knowing that the South is weak in Congress and unable to secure a fair division of the treasury, territory or other property of the United States, have opposed those measures.

In a speech in April 1856, I showed how Congress had, up to June 1846, appropriated in fortifications for defence of Northern more than double the amount expended upon Southern coasts; $10 in Northern to $1 for Southern internal improvements; $4 in Northern to $1 in Southern pensions; two acres of public land for Northern to one for Southern works; $10,000,000 in direct bounties to Northern cod-fishermen, while no Southern industrial interest had any bounty; had built a light for every twenty odd miles of Northern coast, to guide the mariner, while for hundreds of miles of Southern coast not a warning beacon cheered him; and had extorted numberless millions from the South in indirect bounties to Northern manufactures and shipping interests. Northern avarice has striven to appropriate all the lands and most of the other property of the U. S.; Southern ambition has clutched at its highest offices and honors. For the first fifty years of our present government but three Northern men were chosen President—the two Adamses and Van Buren—and each for only one term; while there were five Southern men elected President, each for two terms. But the North has made the South pay dearly for honors in the common treasure and the common territory. I have epitomized an exhibit of the unequal division of treasure. A yet larger share of territory has been appropiated by the North.

The anti-slavery agitation originated in Northern avarice, and has been kept up to serve that passion. It is usual to date its birth from the Missouri restriction; but it was born before the Union and will, I fear, survive it. Pending the Revolution, the North-western territory, belonging to Virginia, excited "the lucrative desires" of the North-eastern people (as Mr. Madison said) to a degree threatening the Confederacy. At the conclusion of the peace of '83, the North had but 164,081 square miles—the South 647,202 square miles of territory. To satisfy those desires and consolidate the Union, Virginia gave all the North-western territory to the Confederacy, and the ordinance of '87 secured it all to the North, by prohibiting slavery therein forever. Thereby the North grew to 425,761 sq. ms. and the South shrank to 385,521 square miles. This was the first step of Abolition, and first *intervention* by Congress against slavery. The territory of Louisiana, next acquired, was, by the Missouri restriction, so partitioned, that the North took (exclusive of Oregon) 659,138 square miles and the South 225,456 square miles. This was the second bold stride of Ablition and *intervention* by Congress against slavery. The acquisitions of Oregon, Florida and Texas, were so divided that the North got 415,467 square miles, the South 271,268 square miles. This was the the third advance of Abolition and *intervention* by Congress against slavery.

The Mexican conquests engrossed by the North added to her limits 587,648 square miles. This was the boldest and longest step yet made by Abolition, if as now maintained by nearly all the North, the *non-intervention*, then inaugurated, *means permissive intervention by squatter-sovereigns against slavery.*

The South has grown from 647,202 to 882,245 square miles; having added but 235,043 square miles to her area since '83. In the same time the North has grown from 164,081 square miles, to 2,088,014 square miles; having added 1,923,933 square miles to her limits. These estimates may not be precisely accurate, but closely approximate the truth.

All this was the fruit of concessions by the South to the North, called compromises—made to secure peace and rest for the South and fraternal concord, harmony and love between North and South! All was claimed by the North to *protect her rights*, or the "rights of freemen and free labor." In the same spirit they claimed *protection* for all Northern industrial interests—manufactures, fisheries, ship-building, coasting trade, &c., by *protective* tariffs, bounties and monopolies, at the expense of slave labor.

In proof, hear an extract from the address of the "Home League," in 1842:

"Now, neither the farmer nor mechanic are contented "to be disfranchised, and debaned the privileges of free- "men, whilst a portion of their countrymen, possessing "a sure market for the products of their slaves, deny "them the right of living by free-labor, unless reduced "to the degradation of working for the same miserable "subsistence allowed to slaves. Even viewed *constitu- "tionally, the owner* of a thousand slaves, *chattels of "industry, or labor-saving machines* as they are called "at the South (!), has surely no more right to be *pro- "tected* than the free-farmer, with a thousand cattle, or "the free manufacturer, with a thousand looms, *chattels "of industry.*

"*Protection is due to all*—we mean *adequate, posi- "tive protection*, whether it is by favorable climate, or "a peculiar chartered grant, or *a discriminating tariff.* "WHEREVER LABOR, the great element of our growth, "and independence *as a nation*, REQUIRES SECURITY "AND PROTECTION, THERE THE PROTECTING HAND OF GOV- "ERNMENT SHOULD BE STRETCHED OUT, with a wise be- "neficence. Let this principle be adopted, and steadily "adhered to, and *there will be an end to any invidious "interference of one portion of our citizens, with the "rights and privileges of the other. We urgently en- "treat our Southern friends, seriously, to take this "view of the subject.*"

Mark and ponder those wise and just sentiments: "*Protection is due to all*". * * "*wherever labor*" * * "*requires security and protection, there* THE PROTECTING HAND OF GOVERNMENT *should be stretched out.*" Now consider the perverted use of those sound sentiments.—It is not meant that our federal government should give *protection to all*, or that *its protecting hand should be stretched out to shelter and secure all our citizens in the enjoyment of what belongs to them—their men-servants and maid-servants as well as cattle and looms. That is all I ask for the South*, but that will not satisfy the North. Its *protection* just read, means, being interpreted, this: "Southern friends, if you will pay a tax on all the salt, your families, slaves and cattle consume, to be given as bounty to our fishermen for catching cod—pay our ship-masters for carrying your cotton, rice or sugar to New York, double the freight an English vessel would charge—pay our manufacturers from fifty to five hundred per cent. more for

Mr. Stuart of Mich. Such is the history of that Proviso, which passed without any public discussion; and which neither altered nor qualified the "intent and meaning' of the act as previously expressed. Such is the substance of Mr. B.'s subsequent explanation of it. We did not and do not ask Congress to legislate slavery into any Territory, or to enact a "slave code" as Mr. Douglas and Black Republicans allege.—Neither do we ask, as the North has too often and too successfully done, protection of our property by taxing others to swell our profits (as by fishing bounties or coast-trade or ship building monopolies,) or by prohibiting others from entering the territories with us (as by Ordinances of '87 or Restrictions of 1820,) but only protection against robbery, fraud, or "unfriendly legislation."

Again we are told that the "National Democratic Convention" at Cincinnati, in '56, pledged us to the Douglas theory of Congressional non-intervention to protect Southern property against Squatter spoliation. If his Southern supporters do not beware how they echo such assertions, they will make a confession of Abolition faith. That Platform proclaims—"Non-interference by Congress with Slavery in State and Territory, and in the District of Columbia." Can the inhabitants of the District (which has no legislature or legislative power,) in virtue of some inherent, or Heaven born sovereignty, rise in their majesty, and, by their declared will, liberate all the slaves therein—whether of inhabitants, or of Congressmen sojourning there? And is Congress pledged by its Nebraska Kansas act, and are its Democratic members pledged by that Platform, not to intervene to protect? Then, indeed, will be accomplished the oft-repeated wish, that I have read and heard, from Abolitionists, of 'severing the National [as they call it] Government from all connection with slavery,—as Mr. Sumner expressed it, 'erasing the blot of Slavery from our National brow.'

The black republicans will all shake hands with the South on this. The Cincinnati Platform proves to much against us, I trow, even in the opinion of Southern anti-Protectionists, if Congress cannot stay the hands of Abolition in the District. If they can popularize this idea, then Abolition will soon achieve its declared purpose—"write in letters of flashing fire, over the gateway of the National Capitol, 'No admittance for Slavery." If this construction of the Non-intervention of that Platform be correct, the South cannot stand on it; it will fall unless braced by some other plank. Until this defect was pointed out by Mr. Douglas and recognized by Southern men, I had regarded it as sound beyond doubt! I tho't it meant the non-intervention of the Kansas act—that Congress should not legislate slavery into or out of any State or Territory or out of the District of Columbia—and only recognized the right of inhabitants of a Territory to exclude Slavery when prepared by numbers to claim admission into the Union and forming a Constitution for their future State. That is my reading and interpretation. I know that it does use these words: "that every citizen and every section of the country has a right to demand and insist upon an equality of rights and privileges, and to complete and ample protection of persons and property from domestic violence and foreign aggression," and I have yet to learn that Southern men and their property are excepted, or may not claim protection by the federal government, in the territories, as well as the District of Columbia, or elsewhere, within federal jurisdiction.

Some demagogue may ask, will you *force slavery on an unwilling people*? Will you not let the majority of the residents in a territory exercise that great American right of self-government, through their agent, the legislature, by excluding slavery? I reply to both questions, no. And these are my reasons. To define property, or declare what shall, or shall not, be property, or to confiscate property, is an attribute of sovereignty. It does not belong to our free republican governments, either Federal or State, much less to our dependent territorial governments. Your Legislature cannot abolish slavery, for it is not sovereign. It can only be done by the only sovereignty we recognize, the people, acting through a Convention in forming their organic law. It cannot be done by Congress, for it has less power over property than your Legislature, and is more restricted by its charter, the Constitution. Least of all can it be done by a territorial legislature, for it is but the servant of servants, subordinate to the will of Congress, which is the creature of the States, and subordinate to their will, the Constituti n of the United States. Until it becomes a State, the territory is the common property of all the States, in which each has an undivided equal part, and equal right of possession, use and enjoyment, with every other State. Until they form a State of the territory, they can no more exclude any State, or the people thereof, and their property, from it, than the tenant can expel or exclude his landlord. If this was a *National* instead of a federal government, formed by *an American Nation*, instead of separate, independent nations or States, for *national* purposes, instead of federal, then there would be reason for insisting that the will of the majority of the inhabitants of a territory, should prevail even to the exclusion of the property of the minority. But such is not the fact: the general government is not National, but federal, the will of the numerical majority of the people of the Union does not prevail, unless the will of the numerical majority of States consent; and the will of both combined cannot prevail over any reserved right of the smallest State or of its humblest citizen. The federal government was not formed on the principle of "the greatest good to the greatest number," or "the right of the majority to govern." If then the territories belong to the States of the Union, they should be governed in the spirit of the federal Constitution, for the common or equal use and benefit of each and every State; and no majority of inhabitants, however great, can violate the reserved rights of the least State or its citizen. Whatever a citizen of any State may hold as property therein, he may hold as property in a territory till it becomes a State. To contend for a territorial Legislative power to confiscate or abolish or exclude his property, is to contend for not merely self-government for the inhabitants, but power to govern the States—their landlords who own the territory!

Neither the Kansas act, nor the Cincinnati Platform, recognize such sovereign power in territorial Legislatures. They admit, as Mr. Buchanan did, in accepting, that platform and the nomination for President—"that the people of a territory, like those of a State, shall decide for themselves whether slavery shall or shall not exist within their limits." As I have said, the sovereign people may do so, by a convention, but their servant, a State Legislature, cannot. In like manner, when the residents of a territory have the requisite numbers to form a State, and become a *people* in the *political sense of that word,* they may in their Constitution exclude slavery from their future State.—This was what Mr. Buchanan meant, as explained in his Inaugural Address, when he said of this territorial power over slavery, "it is a judicial question which legitimately belongs to the Supreme Court of the U. S., before whom it is now pending and will, it is understood, be speedily and finally settled. To their decision in common with all good citizens, I shall cheerfully submit, whatever this may be, though it has ever been my individual opinion, that, under the Nebraska-Kansas act, the appropriate period will be when the number of actual residents in the territory shall justify the formation of a Constitution with a view to its admission as a State into the Union." The Supreme Court did decide, that any citizen has a right to carry slaves into and hold them in a territory, by virtue of the Constitution, and that Congress is pledged by that Constitution to *protect* that property.

Yet, many good citizens, even in the South, insist that Congress shall not discharge its Constitutional duty, because they say it has pledged itself by the Kansas act not to intervene to protect slave property! Can Congress relieve itself from its constitutional obligations at discretion? Can any or all parties relieve it of this obligation? Can the great Democratic Party grant me indulgence for disloyalty to my State, to my conscience, to my God, in not observing my oath to support that Constitution and abetting its violation by Squatter Sovereigns who may defy its authority!! No aspirant for the Presidency, and no party, shall, for the sake of the Presidency or the Union, intervene between me and my God, my conscience or my State.—I cannot sit still, as your Senator and countenance the destruction of your rights of property, to preserve which the Constitution was framed and the Union was formed, until convinced that squatter-sovereignty is superior to the Constitution. Mr. Douglas did not quite assert that in the Senate last winter or before the people of Illinois, in '57;* but his position was more indefensible and inexcusable. According to my understanding, it was this: Conceding the right to carry slave property into the territory and the obligation of the Federal Government to protect it, and that Congress can confer and a territorial Government derive from it no power to exclude slavery, and that the territorial government has no greater or other power than it derives from Congress, yet he maintains that the territorial Legislature may rightfully, by non-action or unfriendly legislation, prevent the holding of such property in the territory.

This doctrine carries its condemnation on its face. It assumes that the legislature may do covertly or indirectly, what it cannot do openly or directly! This is as bad in morals as in politics. I have never heard of anything to warrant it in the political or moral code of any country, worthy of the pen of history, save that of crafty and treacherous Sparta, where theft was applauded, if successfully concealed. What treachery, as well as mockery, to invite Southern men to come with their property into the common territories of the States, under the solemn guarantees of protection of a common Constitution, with a knowledge or belief that squatter-sovereignty may cunningly and rightfully exclude or abolish their property! It reminds me of the philanthropic and patriotic wish of Mr. Corwin, after our gallant soldiers crossed the Rio Grande—'that the Mexicans might welcome them, with bloody hands, to hospitable graves!'

It is revolutionary doctrine, striking at the foundation of all government. Property is the basis of the social fabric. To protect and preserve it, is the chief end of every government. In a state of nature, each man is lord of himself and his possessions, subject to no power but that of his God, and equal to the greatest of men. For what purpose does he yield to the government of men? For the better protection of his person and other property. Property is essential to life, for man cannot live without food and raiment—to liberty, for no restraint is so tyrannous and painful as that of hunger and cold—to happiness, for there can be no enjoyment where the wants of nature are not supplied. I may, therefore, say that property is clothing, iron or wooden utensils, for field or fireside, than French or English would ask—buy all ships, boats or other water-craft of us, at our price—improve our harbors and rivers, as we desire—and give to free-soil and free-labor all the territories of the United States,—we will not interfere with slavery in the Southern States, but will protect it therein, by letting it alone. That is the *adequate, positive protection* promised the South, by those who spoke of this confederacy of States *"as a nation"* and plumed themselves on being *National* Whigs! Such is now, we are told, *the best we can get from Congress!*

I have received many such appeals for *protection* to Northern industry; sometimes, I regret to say, from those calling themselves Democrats. By striving to prevent wasteful expenditures, by unconstitutional appropriations for rivers, harbor and like works, pensions, ocean mails, insane asylums, agricultural colleges, free farms for free labor, free schooling for free Africans, and such measures of miscalled *protection* of industry; and by claiming *adequate protection* to Southern labor—that is, prevention by Congress of robbery or theft of Southern property in States and territories—I have been justly proscribed as not a *national* Democrat, and unjustly assailed as an ultraist, extremist, abstractionist, sectionalist and disorganizer, wanting in expansive patriotism! I shall, probably, bear these opprobious names to my grave; yet, God knows, I have spoken and acted for conscience and my countrys, sake—including all the United States.

But the worst ever said of me is, that by my vote for the Nebraska-Kansas act, I surrendered the constitutional right of the people of Alabama to *protection* by Congress of their property in the common territories, to the discretion of squatter-sovereignty! I repel the charge as false and slanderous. Offensive to me as this charge is, it gives me less pain, than to hear my constituents say 'well done; bad as squatter-sovereignty is, it cannot be worse than intervention by Congress; we are all pledged by the Cincinnati platform to *non-intervention* by Congress, even to protect: for peace and party's sake, let us surrender that *abstract* right and hush agitation.' Ignorant or corrupt servants may be supplanted by wiser and better men; but what hope is there for the country when the people become so demoralized and debased as to fear to demand their acknowledged rights!

The whole history of Congressional action, touching the territories and slavery, negatives the construction, lately given by Judge Douglas and his followers to the Nebraska-Kansas act, while it teaches by example, the folly of yielding rights for the sake of peace and the Union.

The South for her own peace and quiet and the Union, submitted to positive *intervention by Congress* against her, in *prohibiting* Slavery in all the North West Territory—in La. territory North of 36°30'—in Oregon territory—in Texas, north of that line—and according to the Douglas construction agreed to *intervention* against slavery in all Mexican territory, by *Congressional Agents*, the inhabitants thereof: whereby she has given up of her exclusive territory to the North, 261,671 square miles, of other *slave-holding* territory, belonging in common to all the States 972,005 square miles, and in slave-holding and non-slaveholding territory, 1,923,933 square miles, —an empire twelvefold greater than all the Northern States at the peace of '83. *The Northern States never ceded or yielded one foot of territory to the United States.* The South for the sake of peace, quiet and the Union, has submitted to intervention in her domestic affairs against her by collections and disbursements of revenue under laws as iniquitions and oppressive as those of any Kingdom of Europe. For illustration, you have been taxed on all your salt to raise a bounty for New England codfishermen to an amount exceeding $13,000,000; you are not allowed to send a bale of cotton to New York or bring a box of goods back, in any foreign vessel; or buy a foreign vessel for that purpose. But have all these concessions given us peace or saved us from anti-slavery agitation, wrong and injury? No. In the 1st Congress of the Union (1790) petitions praying the abolition of slavery were presented, and have been renewed, at short intervals, ever since. A large majority of Northern Congressmen insisted on *intervention* by Congress against the admission of Missouri, in 1820, in violation of the Missouri restriction, miscalled compromise, and she was at last, gotten into the Union by stratagem. A large minority of Northern Congressmen urged like *intervention* against admitting Ark., and Fla., and a large majority against admitting Texas.

In the meantime, the first general abolition society, was formed in 1832, in Boston, and the second, in 1833, in New York—each pledging its members to labor for *"the abolition of slavery in the U S.*, and the elevation of free negroes to *"equal civil and political rights and privileges with the whites,"* and, for those ends to strive to *"get the subject of slavery fully before Congress,"* and, thro' it, abolish slavery in the District of Columbia, and the inter-state Slave trade, and prohibit it in the Territories. They besieged Congress with petitions, which, in 1836, were so numerous and offensive to the South, that her representatives demanded and obtained the adoption of the famous 21st rule, "that no petition, memorial, or other paper, praying the abolition of slavery in the District of Columbia or any State or Territory, or the slave trade between the States and territories of the U. S., in which it now exists, *shall be received by this House, or entertained in any way whatever."*—Abolition did not abandon the *abstract* right of petition, even to destroy our practical right to life or property, but encouraged by the concessions of such leading Southrons as Clay, of Ky., and Benton of Missouri, continued to clamor for freedom of petition," till 3rd December, '44, when on motion of J. Q. Adams (the most vindictive of Southern foes) the rule was rescinded with the help of Southern votes! Grant the *abstract* right of petition (we were told) and the North will be satisfied and abolition will die of starvation. The next Congress showed the falseness of such predictions, and your then representative (Hon. R. Chapman) vainly tried to renew the rule. Abolition beat him, with the aid of Southern votes, and has ever since sat, with confident security and insolent power, in the very citadel of our Constitutional rights, in view of Virginia, the largest slaveholding state, and in the midst of the slaveholders of the District, scattering "firebrands, arrows and death" throughout the South. The South is paying, annually, into the federal treasury three dollars to one paid by the North for printing, publishing and circulating among us incendiary documents tending to excite arson, murder and insurrection. Thus, we suffered Abolition to achieve its primary object by getting "the subject of Slavery fully before Congress." The Wilmot proviso passed the House of Representatives, in 1847, with but three dissenting votes from the North—in order to forestall us from any share of Mexican territory acquired by Treaty of 2d February 1848—declaring "there shall be neither slavery nor involuntary servitude in any territory on the continent of America, which shall hereafter be acquired by, or annexed to, the U. S." &c. But for the aid of Northern Democratic votes in the Senate, that would then have been made the law of the land. Here was *intervention* attempted by Congress against the South. Deserted even by our allies, the Democracy of the North, we barely succeeded in defeating that Proviso, till 1850, when, in consideration of concessions by the South, the cost of which is yet untold and incalculable, she obtained from the North the last Compromise—the last "final adjustment." For these great concessions the South *got the pledge of non-intervention* by Congress with Slavery in the territories of New Mexico and Utah, and a new *fugitiveslave act. What did that non-intervention mean?* What was the wrong it was intended to remedy? *Intervention* by Congress against slavery as in the North West territory, by the Ordinance *of '87, in the a. territory by the Missouri restriction of '20, in Texan territory by like restriction in '45* Oregon territory by like restriction in 8—*intervention* by refusing admission Missouri, in 1820, in restricting admission, of Arkansas in 1836, of Florida, and of Texas, in 1845, because they were slaveholding. The act of grace towards the South was, pledging Congress not to *intervene*, to preclude or exclude slavery from the territories of New Mexico and Utah in their organic laws or refuse admission to States formed out of them, because they were slaveholding. This was the interpretation given by Southern supporters of those clauses, providing "that the legislative power of the territory shall extend to all rightful subjects of legislation consistent with the Constitution of the U. S.. and the provisions of this act" and "said territory, or any portion of the same, shall be received into the Union, with or without slavery, as their Constitution may prescribe at the time of admission" and "that the Constitution and laws of the U. S., not locally inapplicable shall have the same force and effect within said territory as elsewhere within the U S.," Southern opponents of that compromise. objected not only that the South conceded too much, but got nothing save the fugitive slave act and the bare promise of the North not to prevent slavery in State or territory formed of Utah and New Mexico by Congressional intervention. But, that was thought by some to be worth a great deal, because it *secured the right to carry slaves into them.* When it was suggested, that squatter sovereigns might deny that right by territorial legislation, it was replied, oh! no, it would not be "*rightful* legislation, *consistent with the Constitution.*" Such became throughout the South the accepted construction of the *non-intervention* of the Compromise measures. It was to right the wrong, or cure the mischief, of Congress legislating *against* slavery in organizing territories or rejecting States. In accordance with this idea of non-intervention, it was introduced into the Nebraska-Kansas act of 1854. In it were inserted the provisions just quoted, and another repealing the Missouri restriction, and defining non-intervention, as follows:

> "That the Constitution and laws of the U. S., not locally inapplicable, shall have the same force and effect with in said territory as elsewhere except the 8th section of the act preparatory to the admission of Missouri into the Union, approved March 6, 1820, which being *inconsistent with the principle of non-intervention* by Congress with slavery in the States and territories, as *recognized by the legislation of 1850, commonly called* the Compromise Measures, is hereby declared inoperative and void; it being *the true intent and meaning of this act, not to legislate slavery into any territory or State nor to exclude it therefrom, but to leave the people thereof perfectly free to form and regulate their domestic institutions in their own way, subject only to the Constitution of the U. S.;* Provided, that nothing herein contained shall be construed to revive or put in force any law or regulation which may have existed *prior to the act of 6 March, 1820, either protecting,* establishing, prohibiting or abolishing slavery.'

Here, the wrong to be remedied was Congressional *intervention* against slavery, by the Missouri restriction, which embraced the very

www.ingramcontent.com/pod-product-compliance
Lightning Source LLC
LaVergne TN
LVHW020643110826
845149LV00004B/1336

* 9 7 8 1 4 1 8 1 8 9 8 7 7 *